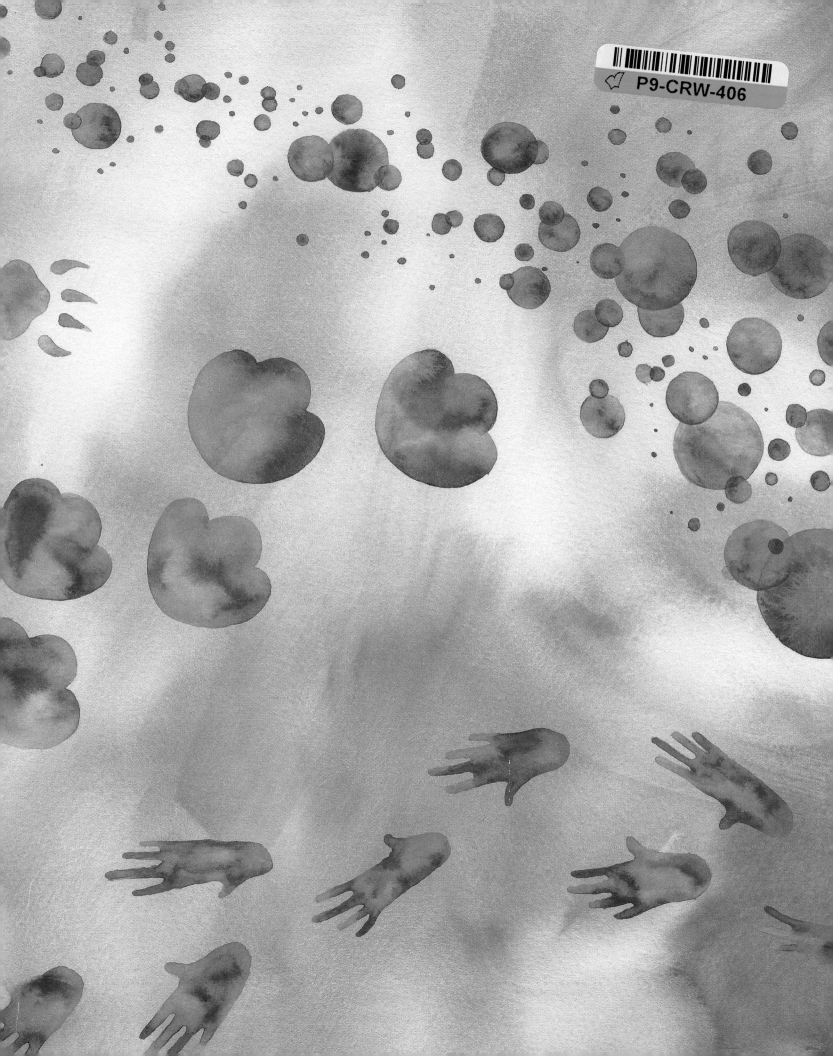

P9-CRW-406

DON'T
Let Them
DISAPPEAR

12 Endangered Species Across the Globe

Written by
Chelsea Clinton

Illustrated by
Gianna Marino

PHILOMEL BOOKS

For Charlotte, Aidan and
all children, who deserve
to grow up in a world where
no animal is endangered
—C.C.

In loving memory of my
father, who taught me to
love all the animals
—G.M.

PHILOMEL BOOKS
An imprint of Penguin Random House LLC
New York

Text copyright © 2019 by Chelsea Clinton. Illustrations copyright © 2019 by Gianna Marino.

Penguin supports copyright. Copyright fuels creativity, encourages diverse voices, promotes free speech, and creates a vibrant culture. Thank you for buying an authorized edition of this book and for complying with copyright laws by not reproducing, scanning, or distributing any part of it in any form without permission. You are supporting writers and allowing Penguin to continue to publish books for every reader.

Philomel Books is a registered trademark of Penguin Random House LLC.

Visit us online at penguinrandomhouse.com

Library of Congress Cataloging-in-Publication Data is available upon request.
Manufactured in the United States of America.
ISBN 9780525514329
1 3 5 7 9 10 8 6 4 2

Edited by Jill Santopolo. • Design by Ellice M. Lee.
Text set in ITC Caslon. • The art was done in gouache on Fabriano watercolor paper.

There are animals on every continent and in every ocean on Earth. Tall ones and short ones. Massive ones and smaller ones. Animals with long necks and long legs, animals that are strong and not so strong. Every animal species is unique and important to life on Earth. Some are almost gone and could become extinct if we don't act now to save them.

KEY

Some animals are more in danger of disappearing than others. Conservationists who study endangered animals classify the level of their risk of extinction. On the scale of not endangered to extinct:

Not Vulnerable: Most animals—though every year, more species are added to the categories below

Nearly Vulnerable: Animals that are on their way to having fewer than 10,000 left

Vulnerable: Fewer than 10,000 left—if nothing is done, they could be extinct in the wild within 100 years

Endangered: Fewer than 2,500 left—if nothing is done, they could be extinct in the wild within 20 years

Critically Endangered: Fewer than 250 left—if nothing is done, they could be extinct in the wild within 10 years

Extinct in the Wild: Animals live only in captivity

Extinct: No remaining animals on Earth

Long before the sun is up, **GIRAFFES** wake early to get a head start on the day's work of walking, eating and staying away from predators. Towers of giraffes will walk nine miles or more every day to find all the food they need to eat. Even though they are the tallest animals on Earth, with the longest necks, they use their nearly two-foot-long tongues to reach even higher for the leaves that make up most of their diet. Every giraffe has a unique pattern of spots to help hide from predators. But giraffes don't rely solely on their spots for protection. A single giraffe kick can kill a lion!

Don't let them disappear!

Range: Central, Eastern and Southern Africa

Endangered Status: Vulnerable

Why: Habitat destruction, poaching, war and climate change

Range: Central sub-Saharan Africa

Endangered Status: Critically Endangered

Why: Habitat destruction, poaching and war

Waking up with the sun, GORILLAS leave their nests to find food before they'll need to rest again as the day heats up. While gorillas mainly eat plants, they sometimes snack on small insects, too. It's hard work gathering the dozens of pounds of food that adult gorillas need to consume each day! Gorilla moms carry their babies on their chests or backs, and a troop of gorillas communicates by using sounds and facial expressions, similar to the way we do. In captivity, some gorillas have even been taught to use sign language. Language is not the only thing humans and gorillas share—gorillas can also catch human diseases, even a cold, which can be deadly.

Don't let them disappear!

BLUE WHALES are the largest animals the world has ever seen. Whales are mammals, like us; but unlike us, blue whales have to focus on breathing, which means they can never be fully asleep. They take in oxygen from water and air, and when they breathe out, the vapor can soar up to thirty feet high, making them visible, including to the whalers who almost hunted them to extinction fifty years ago. They tend not to travel in big pods—preferring to swim alone or in pairs. That doesn't mean they're not in touch, though. Blue whales communicate with one another up to a thousand miles away, at a frequency too low for humans to hear and in a language scientists are still working to understand. But scientists can sense their heartbeats from up to twenty miles away.

Don't let them disappear!

Range: Every ocean except the Arctic

Endangered Status: Endangered

Why: Historically, hunting; now, with
hunting outlawed, blue whale
numbers are growing

By the time the sun comes up,
RHINOCEROSES have long been grazing.
Sleeping only during the hottest periods of the day, rhinos
spend most of their time eating or rolling in mud to stay cool.
The mud also acts as sunscreen and shields rhinos' skin from bugs.
While rhinos spend little time together in a crash, or a group, they
are often found in the company of oxpeckers, which are birds that
sit on rhinos' backs eating bugs. Oxpeckers also warn rhinos if
danger is approaching. That's particularly helpful to rhinos because
their eyesight isn't very good (though their senses of smell and
hearing are strong). Rhinos have very thick skin, and their horns
are made from keratin, just like our fingernails and hair.

Don't let them disappear!

Range: Eastern and Southern Africa, Northern India, Southern Nepal, Indonesia and Malaysia

Endangered Status:

Critically Endangered: Black rhinos, Sumatran rhinos, Javan rhinos and northern white rhinos

Nearly Vulnerable: Southern white rhinos

Vulnerable: Indian rhinos

Why: Poaching and habitat loss

Range: Central China

Endangered Status: Vulnerable

Why: Habitat loss

Although GIANT PANDAS spend most of their time alone, in the afternoon you might find an embarrassment of giant pandas eating lots of bamboo together. They need to eat so much bamboo—more than twenty-five pounds a day!—because it's not very nutritious. Unlike other bears, giant pandas do not hibernate or roar—but they do squeak and growl and use scents to communicate with one another. While they're born pink, the distinctive black and white fur they later grow is a form of camouflage, helping giant pandas blend in with shadows in their native bamboo forests. They rarely need the camouflage, though, since they have very few animal predators.

Don't let them disappear!

WHALE SHARKS are the biggest fish in the world and may be one of the few animals who never sleep, no matter what time of day or night it is. From the moment they're born, whale sharks never stop swimming. Alive when dinosaurs roamed the earth, sharks have been around for hundreds of millions of years. They don't have a single bone in their bodies; whale shark skeletons are made up of cartilage—the same substance that's in our noses and ears. No matter where they are, shivers of whale sharks can sense a drop of blood if it's in the water nearby, though they eat mainly plankton.

Don't let them disappear!

Range: Close to the Equator in oceans worldwide
Endangered Status: Endangered
Why: Hunting, collisions with boats and being
　　　trapped in fishing nets

In the Arctic, for much of the year, day and night do not have the same meaning they do in other places on Earth. In the summer, it's light for nearly twenty-four hours a day; in the winter, it's dark all day. Celebrations of **POLAR BEARS** sleep when seals, their main food, are sleeping. Most of their seal hunting takes place underwater. To withstand below-freezing temperatures above and below water, polar bears have two layers of fur. Their fur gives them their whitish coloring; their skin is black. Polar bears have good eyesight to help distinguish different shades of white on the ice and can smell seals up to twenty miles away.

Don't let them disappear!

Range: The Arctic across the United States (Alaska), Canada, Denmark (Greenland), Norway and Russia

Endangered Status: Vulnerable

Why: Climate change, habitat loss and less prey to eat

Range: Sub-Saharan Africa, India

Endangered Status:

    Endangered: Asiatic lions

    Vulnerable: African lions

Why: Conflict with human neighbors, less prey
    to eat, poaching and habitat loss

As the sun begins to set, LIONESSES head
out to hunt antelopes, buffalo, wildebeest, zebra and giraffes
to feed their pride. But they don't hunt all day; lionesses can sleep
for more than fifteen hours each day. Male LIONS sleep even longer, up
to twenty hours a day, even though they rarely hunt. Both lions and lionesses
will fight to protect their pride. A male lion's mane provides extra protection
and also shows how old a lion is—the darker the mane, the
older the lion. Lions and lionesses communicate with
one another in many ways, including by roaring.
A lion's roar can be heard from five miles away,
helping members of their pride who might have
wandered off to find their way back or helping
hunters find them. Even though they're called the
king of the jungle, they're still not safe from harm.

Don't let them disappear!

A romp of **SEA OTTERS** settles down to sleep by lying on their backs and wrapping themselves in kelp so they don't have to worry about floating out to sea. If there's no kelp nearby, and sometimes even if there is, otters will join together, making a raft for stability and security. Sea otters use rocks to crack open the clams and other shellfish they like to eat. If a sea otter finds a particularly useful rock, it will travel with it and use it over and over again. After every meal, sea otters wash their paws and fur, no easy task given that they have more hair on a small patch of skin than we have on our heads!

Don't let them disappear!

Range: Across the North Pacific Ocean (from Japan and
Russia to the United States and Canada, possibly as
far south as Mexico)

Endangered Status: Endangered

Why: Pollution, less prey to eat, habitat loss and poaching

Range: Sumatra
(Indonesia) and
Borneo (Indonesia
and Malaysia)
Endangered Status: Critically
Endangered
Why: Habitat loss and poaching
(Bornean orangutans only)

As the sun sets, ORANGUTANS prepare nests in the trees, sometimes building roofs to cover the mattresses they have woven out of branches and leaves. Like us, orangutans prefer to sleep in protected spaces. Unlike us, their arms are longer than their bodies, to help them navigate from branch to branch, tree to tree. Orangutans tend to spend more time on their own than in groups, and much of that time is spent climbing, sitting and swinging high above the ground. When a congress of orangutans is together, they communicate with sounds, facial expressions and gestures, like we do. Their similarities to us are reflected in their name—orangutan means "person of the forest" in Malay, the language spoken in orangutans' native Malaysia.

Don't let them disappear!

When night has fallen, **TIGERS** wake up to hunt. Their night vision is up to six times more powerful than ours is. As the biggest cats on Earth, tigers need a lot of meat to stay healthy and strong. They hunt mainly for deer, wild pigs, antelope and water buffalo. Tigers are good athletes and can jump more than fifteen feet in one pounce and run more than forty miles per hour over short distances. Unlike most other cats, they love water and can swim more than three miles at a time. Generally solitary animals, tiger moms and cubs together form a streak, each with their own distinct pattern of brown, black or gray stripes.

Don't let them disappear!

Range: South and Southeast Asia, China and Russia

Endangered Status: Endangered

Why: Poaching and habitat loss

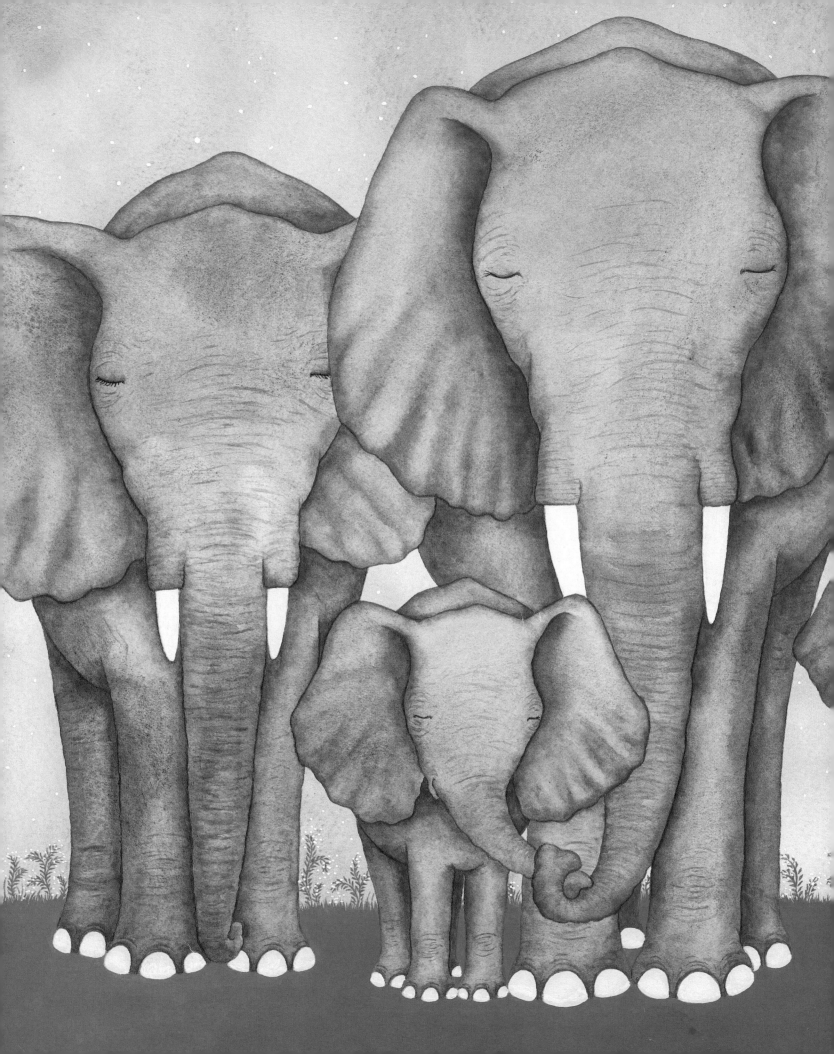

Late at night, ELEPHANT herds are fast asleep, enjoying their second sleep of the day; the first comes when the sun is high and hot. The largest animals on land, elephants have trunks that can weigh 400 pounds and can be more than 6 feet long. Elephants use their trunks to sense an object's size, shape and temperature—and they use them like a snorkel when swimming. All elephants have trunks, but not all elephants have tusks, the very long teeth that help them find food and water. Elephants have a range of emotions like we do, including love, compassion and grief—they even cry over their lost loved ones years after they've gone.

Don't let them disappear!

Range: Sub-Saharan Africa, South and
Southeast Asia
Endangered Status:
Endangered: Asian elephants
Vulnerable: African elephants
Why: Poaching and habitat loss

Let's make a pledge as fellow inhabitants of Planet Earth, *that we won't let any of these species disappear.*

WHY ARE THEY ENDANGERED?

There are many reasons the animals in this book are endangered, which have been highlighted on each page. Here's a bit more information about some of the main ones:

- Global warming leads to warmer oceans and less sea ice, which is a particular challenge for polar bears.
- Water pollution makes it harder for sea otters to find the food they need.
- Overfishing of krill is a challenge for blue whales because there is less of their main source of food.
- Poaching, which is hunting that's against the law, is a threat to all animals that some people think are worth more dead than alive. This includes tigers (whose teeth, eyes and bones are wrongly believed to have magical powers), elephants (whose tusks are prized for their ivory), rhinos (whose horns some people wrongly think have medicinal properties) and mountain gorillas (for their meat).
- Legal hunting is a problem for animals in some places, including whale sharks (which are killed to make shark fin soup) as well as giraffes and lions (which are killed because some people think their heads and tails make great trophies).
- Clearing land for farming and development is shrinking many animals' habitats, including orangutans (whose treetop homes are being cut down for palm oil plantations) and giant pandas (whose bamboo forest homes are being cut down for buildings, homes and roads).

All these things can be changed, though, and if we all work together to make those changes, eventually these animals won't be endangered anymore.

WHAT CAN YOU DO?

If you and your family want to help animals like the ones in this book, here are some things you can do:

- Talk to your friends about the animals in this book and why they're so special.
- Support zoos and visit the animals there.
- Tell your family they shouldn't buy jewelry, trophies or anything else made from endangered animals.
- Recycle whenever you can to help fight global warming.
- Never throw trash in the ocean or anywhere but a recycling bin or trash can.
- Help plant trees in your community to fight climate change.
- Celebrate animals on their special days:

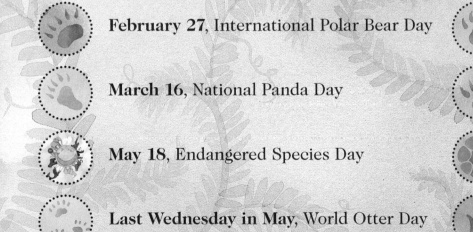

February 27, International Polar Bear Day

March 16, National Panda Day

May 18, Endangered Species Day

Last Wednesday in May, World Otter Day

June 21, World Giraffe Day

July 14, Shark Awareness Day

July 29, International Tiger Day

August 10, World Lion Day

August 12, World Elephant Day

August 19, World Orangutan Day

September 22, World Rhino Day

September 24, World Gorilla Day